ENGINEERING WONDERS

THE PANAMA CANAL

BY REBECCA STEFFOFF

CAPSTONE PRESS
a capstone imprint

Fact Finders Books are published by Capstone Press,
1710 Roe Crest Drive, North Mankato, Minnesota 56003
www.mycapstone.com

Library of Congress Cataloging-in-Publication Data
Names: Stefoff, Rebecca, 1951- author.
Title: The Panama Canal / by Rebecca Stefoff.
Other titles: Fact finders. Engineering wonders.
Description: North Mankato, Minnesota : Capstone Press, [2016] | Series: Fact
    finders. Engineering wonders | Audience: Ages 8–9 | Audience: Grades 4
    to 6 | Includes bibliographical references and index.
Identifiers: LCCN 2015035476
    ISBN 978-1-4914-8198-1 (library binding)
    ISBN 978-1-4914-8202-5 (pbk.)
    ISBN 978-1-4914-8206-3 (ebook pdf)
Subjects: LCSH: Canals—Panama—Design and construction—History—Juvenile
    literature. | Panama Canal (Panama)—Design and
    construction—History—Juvenile literature. | Canal
    Zone--History—Juvenile literature. | Panama—History—20th
    century—Juvenile literature.
Classification: LCC TC774 .S84 2016 | DDC 627/.130972875—dc23
LC record available at http://lccn.loc.gov/2015035476

Editorial Credits
Elizabeth Johnson and Gena Chester, editors; Veronica Scott, designer;
Svetlana Zhurkin, media researcher; Lori Barbeau, production specialist

Photo Credits
Dreamstime: Adeliepenguin, 29 (top); iStockphoto: Danielho, 17, duncan1890, 13, Nancy
Nehring, 11; Library of Congress, cover, 7, 8, 9, 15, 19, 21, 25, 27; Newscom: akg-images, 5
(top); Shutterstock: Arkela, 16, dikobraziy, 10, Everett Historical, 23, Globe Turner, 5 (bottom),
LSkywalker, 22, Peter Hermes Furian, 29 (bottom)

Design Elements by Shutterstock

Printed in the United States of America, in North Mankato.
007539CGS16

TABLE OF CONTENTS

CHAPTER 1

DIGGING ACROSS AMERICA

People cheered wildly as the ship came into sight. Photographers climbed on each other's shoulders to take photos. It was August 15, 1914. A ship called the *Ancon* had just made history. The *Ancon* started the day's journey in the Atlantic Ocean. It sailed into the Pacific Ocean 48 miles (77 kilometers) later. That trip was the first official voyage through the brand-new Panama Canal.

The canal cut across the Americas through the country of Panama, in Central America. For years people had dreamed of the **canal**. The first try at building it had failed. Now, at last, the canal was done!

canal—a canal is a human-made water channel

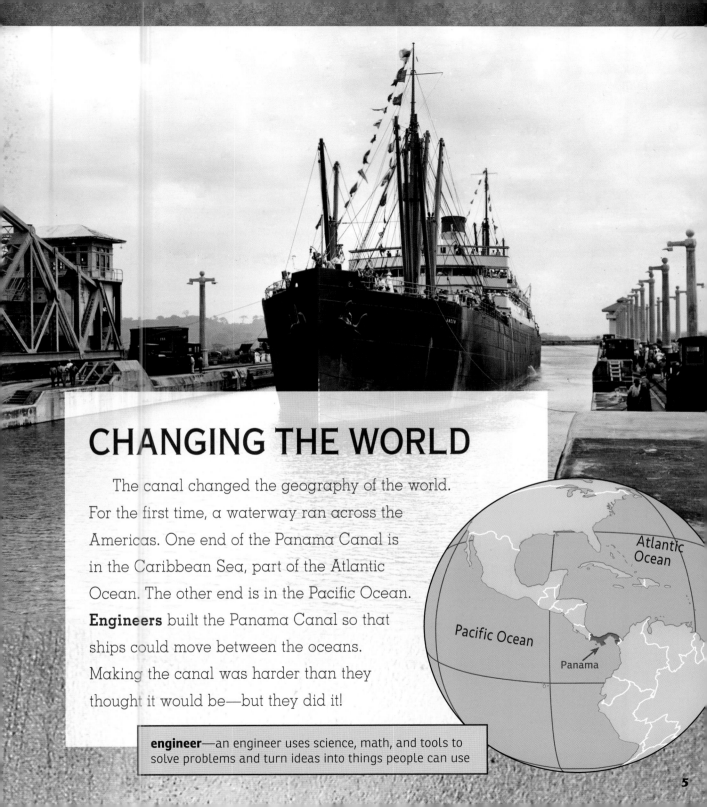

CHANGING THE WORLD

The canal changed the geography of the world. For the first time, a waterway ran across the Americas. One end of the Panama Canal is in the Caribbean Sea, part of the Atlantic Ocean. The other end is in the Pacific Ocean. **Engineers** built the Panama Canal so that ships could move between the oceans. Making the canal was harder than they thought it would be—but they did it!

Atlantic Ocean

Pacific Ocean

Panama

engineer—an engineer uses science, math, and tools to solve problems and turn ideas into things people can use

5

THE BIGGEST JOB

The Panama Canal was the biggest engineering job Americans had ever done. It took 33 years to build the canal. More than 75,000 people worked on it. On the busiest days, up to 25,000 people worked at the same time. To make the Panama Canal, workers moved tons of earth. They moved enough earth to fill 400 Olympic-sized swimming pools.

But building the canal was more than digging a big ditch. The Panama Canal engineers also had to get ships over high hills in the middle of the canal.

Picture a box 3 feet long, 3 feet wide, and 3 feet deep (1 meter on each side). Now imagine packing it full of dirt. Panama Canal workers moved 268 million times that much dirt.

CHAPTER 2

NEEDED: A SHORTCUT FOR SHIPS

A French company started building the Panama Canal in 1881. Work stopped in 1899 when the company ran out of money. Five years later the United States took over. The canal would cost the United States $375 million. Why would two countries try so hard to build the Panama Canal? The answer has to do with geography.

Did You Know?

People started talking about a canal through Central America long before the Panama Canal was built. In 1786, American president Thomas Jefferson thought it was a good idea.

AROUND THE HORN

Before the Panama Canal, there was only one way for ships to go between the Atlantic and Pacific oceans. It was called "rounding the Horn." The tip of South America is called Cape Horn. Ships had to sail around it to go from Europe to Asia, or from California to New York. Rounding the Horn was dangerous. Storms and huge waves battered ships. Many lives and ships were lost.

Gold was found in California in 1849. Miners from Europe and the eastern United States wanted to join the California Gold Rush. An American company built a railroad across Panama to carry those miners.

A SHORTER, SAFER TRIP

A canal through Central America would make the sea voyage shorter and safer. Ships would no longer have to round the Horn. The trip would be 8,000 miles (12,874 km) shorter. A shorter trip would save money for shipping companies. The canal would help them earn money too. Whoever owned the canal could make people pay to use it. The canal would also be important in wartime. Navies could move their ships around the world much faster than before.

THE BEST PLACE FOR A CANAL

Where should the canal be built? Engineers helped answer that question. They studied the landscape and drew plans for canals in several places. Panama was the final choice. It already had a railroad to carry workers and supplies for the canal project. Also, Panama is an **isthmus** and has the shortest distance between the two oceans. Panama was a good choice. Still, building the canal would be full of challenges.

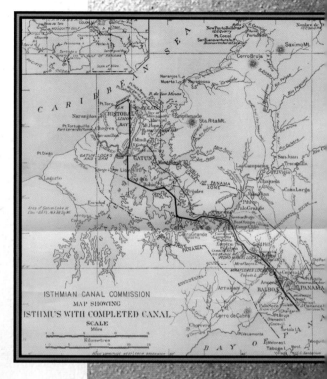

ISTHMIAN CANAL COMMISSION
MAP SHOWING
ISTHMUS WITH COMPLETED CANAL
SCALE
Miles
Kilometres

NOT THE FIRST CANAL

The Panama Canal was not the first canal from one ocean to another. The Suez Canal in Egypt opened in 1869. Using the Suez Canal, ships could move quickly between the Atlantic and Indian oceans. Before the canal, they had to go all the way around Africa. The Suez Canal is more than twice as long as the Panama Canal. Yet the Panama Canal was much harder to build. The Suez Canal goes through flat desert. The Panama Canal was carved through rocky, jungle-covered hills.

isthmus—a narrow strip of land between two bodies of water

11

CHAPTER 3

HOW DO YOU GET A SHIP OVER A MOUNTAIN?

Over the course of the project, engineers came up with two different ways to build a canal through Panama. The first **design** was a flat canal. The second design would take ships up and over the mountains. The project began using the flat canal design.

When the United States took over the project in 1904, the canal builders had to make a choice. Should they stick with the first design? Or should they switch to the second design?

DESIGN ONE: A FLAT CANAL

The first Panama design was flat, like the Suez Canal in Egypt. The Suez Canal is a sea-level canal. The water is at the same level at both ends, and all through the middle. The Suez Canal was built in flat, open desert. It was easy to get workers and machines to the project. The soil was fairly soft and easy to dig.

design—a picture of how a finished project will look, along with a plan for making or building it

The same French company that built the Suez Canal started to work on the Panama Canal. They found that building a sea-level canal is harder if there are rocky jungle hills in the way. First, tens of thousands of trees have to be cut down and moved. Then a channel must be cut through the rock all the way down to **sea level**.

Even after years of work, builders could not dig down to sea level in the hills of Panama. As they dug deeper, landslides dumped tons of dirt and rock back into the canal. Another problem was the Chagres River. During the rainy season it was full and fast. Water rushing into the canal would be a danger to ships.

A bird's-eye view of the flat design used at the Suez Canal.

sea level—the height of the ocean's surface

DESIGN TWO: UP AND OVER

In 1887 engineers came up with a new design for the Panama Canal. It looked like a set of steps going up and down the hills. When the United States decided to buy the canal project, they voted on which design to use. American engineer John Frank Stevens liked the "step" design. His ideas helped the United States choose the second design.

This design called for **dams** to be built. They would tame the Chagres River. Water from the river would form Gatùn Lake at the highest part of the canal. The lake was a key part of the design. Its water would flow down on each side into steps called **locks**.

dam—a barrier built to block a body of water
lock—a pool or chamber with gates to let ships in and out

Each lock could raise or lower a ship to the next step. Together, the locks would form "steps" so that ships could get up and over the highest part of the canal.

Engineers were sure the second design would work. They still had a big job to do. They had to finish the canal.

This infographic shows each step a ship passes through to get up and over the hills in Panama.

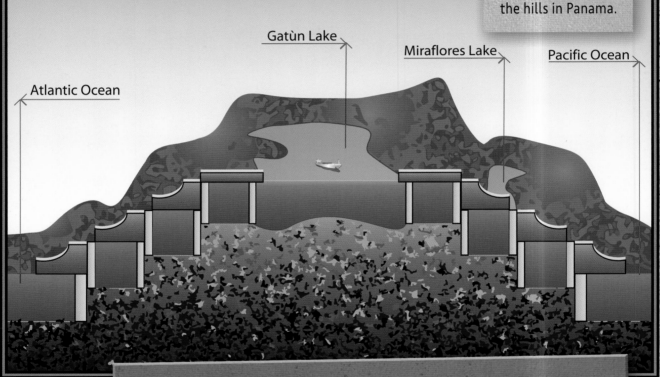

Gatùn Lake

Miraflores Lake

Pacific Ocean

Atlantic Ocean

Did You Know?

When the United States agreed to build the canal, it got control of some land on each side. In 1999, the United States gave the canal and land to Panama. The government of Panama now runs the canal.

RAINFOREST ISLAND

Barro Colorado Island was once the top of a small mountain. When Gatùn Lake formed around it, the mountaintop became an island. Today the island is a nature reserve. It is one of the best places on earth to see a tropical rain forest. Barro Colorado is home to thousands of species of animals, including monkeys, bats, colorful birds, and frogs. Scientists from all over the world have studied wildlife on this island in the Panama Canal.

CHAPTER 4

HUGE TOOLS FOR A HUGE TASK

The builders of the Panama Canal used many kinds of **technology**. Some of their tools were simple. Others were new inventions.

MASSIVE EARTH MOVERS

Digging the canal meant moving tons of earth. Both men and machines did this work.

Men broke up dirt and rock with pickaxes. They shoveled earth into buckets. Lines of men handed the buckets along from one to the next. Dirt was dumped into railroad cars and taken away by train. Workers used dynamite and other explosives to blast through rock. Then they hauled away the broken rock.

Other workers drove machines. The French builders used excavators. These machines had many buckets to scoop up loads of earth. Digging machines called dredges sat on flat boats. The dredges scraped the bottom of the canal to make it deeper.

technology—the use of science to do practical things, such as designing complex machines

American engineers brought big new machines to Panama. More than a hundred steam shovels traveled along the canal on railroad cars. These giant shovels reached out with long metal arms. They carved away chunks of earth. Huge crushers turned boulders into gravel. Steam-powered cranes lifted heavy loads. Some of these were the biggest machines that had ever been made in the United States.

THE BIGGEST LOCKS EVER BUILT

The locks were an important part of the canal. Engineers had built locks before, but never as big as in Panama. The highest point of the canal is Gatùn Lake. It is 85 feet (30 m) above sea level. The locks had to lift ships up to the level of the lake. Then they had to lower the ships back down to sea level.

The Panama Canal has three sets of locks. They form three steps near each end of the canal. The locks are made of concrete. Each lock is 1,050 feet (320 m) long and 110 feet (33.5 m) wide. Every lock has two steel doors called gates. The gates are more than 6 feet (2 m) thick. They are 66 feet (20 m) high. They open to let ships in or out.

The gates are a marvel of engineering. They had to be strong enough to hold back a lot of water. Yet they also had to open and close easily. After more than a hundred years, the gates still work perfectly.

The gates were made of hollow, watertight cells like those found in ships.

Locks are like stairs for ships. Each "step" lifts the ship up or lowers it down. Water flows in and out of locks through openings called valves.

To go up, a ship enters through the lower gate. The gates are closed. The filling valve opens. Water flows in from the next lock up. The ship rises to the level of that lock. The upper gate opens, and the ship moves out.

To go down, the ship enters through the upper gate. Water is pumped out into the next lock down. When the ship is at the level of that lower lock, the lower gate opens. The ship has come down a full "step."

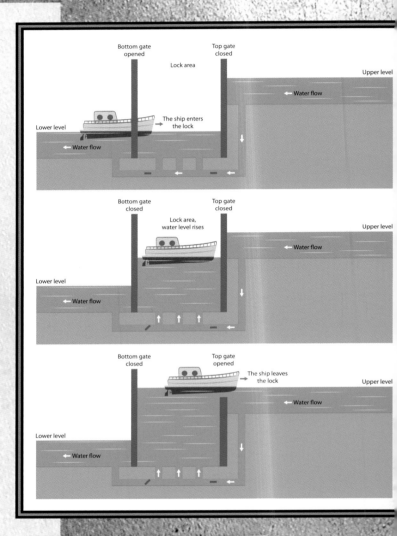

Did You Know?

The people of China built simple locks in rivers 2,000 years ago. Instead of steel gates like the Panama locks, the old Chinese locks had wooden gates.

ELECTRICAL POWER

The Panama Canal was the first canal powered by electricity. The lock system has about 1,500 electric motors. They run on energy made by water flowing through the locks. Electricity also powers the canal's "mules." These are small train engines. They run on tracks beside the locks. When a ship enters a lock, it is tied to a mule on each side. The mules guide the ship to the right place in the lock.

Two workers walk in front of a mule as it leads a ship through the lock.

CHAPTER 5

BEATING SICKNESS AND BLASTING ROCK

Building a canal across Panama was like fighting a war. To win, builders had to defeat two mighty enemies. One was disease. The other was called the Culebra Cut (koo-LEY-bruh KUT).

PANAMA CANAL TIMELINE

1534	**The king of Spain talks about a canal through Panama**
1855	**A railroad across Panama is completed**
1881	**France starts work on the Panama Canal**
1889	**France stops work on the canal**
1904	**The United States starts work on the canal**
1914	**The Panama Canal opens under U.S. control**
1999	**The United States turns the canal over to Panama**
2013	**Panama starts making the canal bigger**

BATTLING DISEASE

More than 25,000 people died while working on the Panama Canal. Accidents killed some workers, but tropical diseases killed thousands more. The worst diseases were malaria and yellow fever.

While the canal was being built, scientists learned something about those diseases. Malaria and yellow fever are spread by mosquito bites. William Gorgas of the U.S. Army used the new knowledge to attack disease in Panama. Gorgas put screens on the doors and windows of the workers' houses. He had workers drain pools of water where young mosquitoes hatched. He sprayed swamps with oil to kill mosquitoes. It worked. After two years there were almost no cases of malaria or yellow fever on the project. People in other tropical lands started doing what Gorgas had done.

THE CULEBRA CUT

The canal route went though a mountain ridge called Culebra. Builders had to cut through the ridge. This part of the canal project was called the Culebra Cut.

The French builders started a narrow cut through the ridge. Landslides were the biggest challenge. Masses of dirt and rock slid down from the top of the ridge. They moved on a layer of slippery clay.

When the Americans took over, they decided to make the cut wider and deeper. If the sides were less steep, there would be fewer landslides. Engineers used strong hoses to wash away the slippery clay. This also meant fewer landslides.

To tackle the cut, engineers built railways around it. Huge steam shovels mounted on train cars rolled up to the work area. Trains also carried away the earth dugs from the cut. The engineers were successful. The Culebra Cut was the hardest part of the canal to dig, but builders finished it in 1913.

Did You Know?

In 1928 an American writer named Richard Halliburton swam through the canal. At that time, boats and ships had to pay a fee based on their weight. Halliburton, at 150 pounds, was charged just 36 cents!

HEAVY TRAFFIC

The builders of the Panama Canal knew it would change how ships move around the world. It is unlikely, though, that they knew just how much difference it would make. A thousand ships used the Panama Canal in its first year. One hundred years later in 2014, more than 13,000 ships used it. Some of those ships carried tourists who were thrilled to see the locks and the Culebra Cut. More than two thirds of the ships carried goods between Asia and the United States.

FIXING THE CANAL FOR THE FUTURE

Today the Panama Canal faces new challenges. The biggest ships that can fit into the Panama Canal locks are called **Panamax**. But some cargo ships and military ships are now bigger than Panamax. They cannot use the Panama Canal. To solve that problem, Panama has built a new set of very large locks at each end of the canal. New channels will guide ships that are bigger than Panamax to these locks.

Panamax—largest ships that can fit into the locks of the Panama Canal

Dredges are at work making the old channel deeper. If all goes well, the new locks will be open in 2016.

The Panama Canal changed the world by connecting two oceans across the Americas. More than 100 years later, Panama's engineers continue their work every day.

A NEW CANAL?

Nicaragua is a country north of Panama. Before the Panama Canal was built, some people thought it should be built in Nicaragua. Now a Nicaragua canal is planned. It will be big enough for the largest ships. Work on the canal started in 2014, but many questions remain. Can Nicaragua pay for the canal? Will the canal hurt protected wildlife and rain forests? How many farmers will lose their land? Only time will tell if the Nicaragua canal will be finished.

GLOSSARY

canal (kuh-NAL)—a human-made water channel that may be large enough for ships to travel on it

dam (DAM)—a barrier built to block a body of water

design (di-ZYN)—a picture of how a finished project or product will look, with a plan for how to build it or make it

engineer (en-juh-NEER)— an engineer uses science, math and tools to solve problems and turn ideas into things people can use

isthmus (ISS-muhss)—a narrow strip of land between two bodies of water

lock (LOK)—a waterproof chamber that can be filled with water to raise a ship or emptied of water to lower a ship

Panamax (pan-uh-MAKS)—largest ships that can fit into the locks of the Panama Canal

sea level (SEE LEV-uhl)—the height or level of the surface of the ocean

technology (tek-NOL-uh-jee)—use of science to do practical things, such as designing complex machines

READ MORE

Benoit, Peter. *The Panama Canal*. New York: Children's Press, 2014.

Brasch, Nicolas. *Triumphs of Engineering*. New York: Rosen Publishing Group, Inc., 2013.

Latham, Donna. *Canals and Dams*. White River Junction, VT: Nomad Press, 2013.

INTERNET SITES

FactHound offers a safe, fun way to find Internet sites related to this book. All of the sites on FactHound have been researched by our staff.

Here's all you do:
Visit *www.facthound.com*
Type in this code: 9781491481981

 Check out projects, games and lots more at **www.capstonekids.com**

CRITICAL THINKING USING THE COMMON CORE

1. What were the two designs for building the Panama Canal? How were they different? List two problems with the first design. (Key Ideas and Details)

2. How important is geography in the story of the Panama Canal? Could the story of building the canal be different if it someone from France told it? What about someone from Panama? (Craft and Structure)

3. What were the results of building the Panama Canal? How has the building of the canal changed world history? (Integration of Knowledge and Ideas)